AREA MAZE MADNESS

Stretch Your Brain with Fun Math and Challenging Logic Puzzles

Graham Jones

ULYSSES PRESS

First published in the UK as *Area² Maze Puzzles* in 2019 by Carlton Books Ltd.

Published in the U.S. by:
ULYSSES PRESS
P.O. Box 3440
Berkeley, CA 94703
www.ulyssespress.com

ISBN: 978-1-61243-942-6
Library of Congress Control Number: 2019942019

10 9 8 7 6 5 4 3 2 1

Printed in Canada by Marquis Book Printing

Acquisitions editor: Casie Vogel
US proofreader: Barbara Schultz
Cover design: David Hastings

PUZZLE 1

The simplest Area Maze possible. Find the length indicated by the question mark.

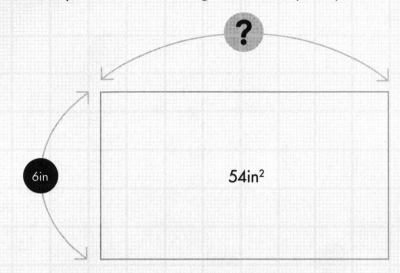

PUZZLE 2

Find the length indicated by the question mark.

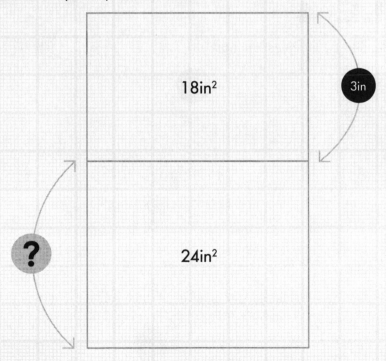

PUZZLE 3

The area of a triangle is the height multiplied by the width, halved. Find the area indicated by the question mark.

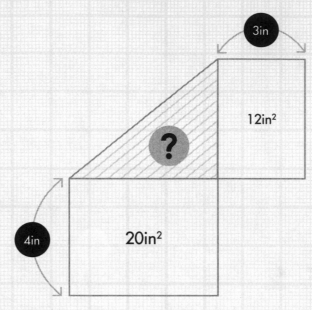

PUZZLE 4

Find the area indicated by the question mark.

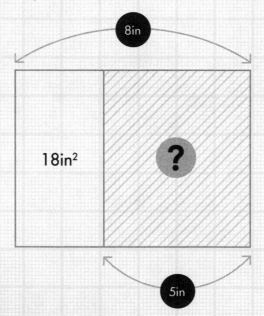

PUZZLE 5

Find the area indicated by the question mark.

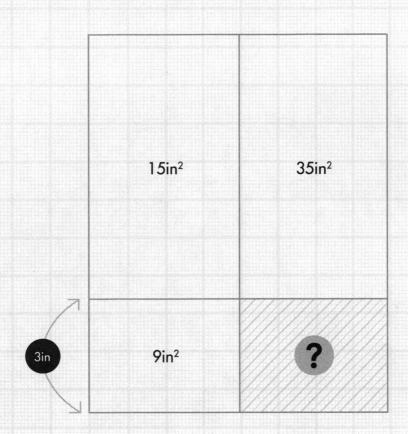

PUZZLE 6

Relative values might be important here.

Find the length indicated by the question mark.

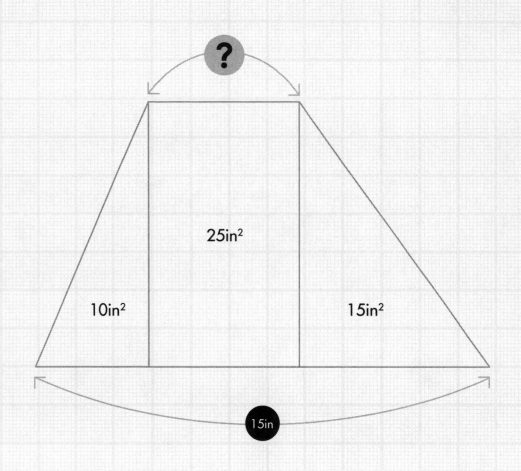

PUZZLE 7

Find the length indicated by the question mark.

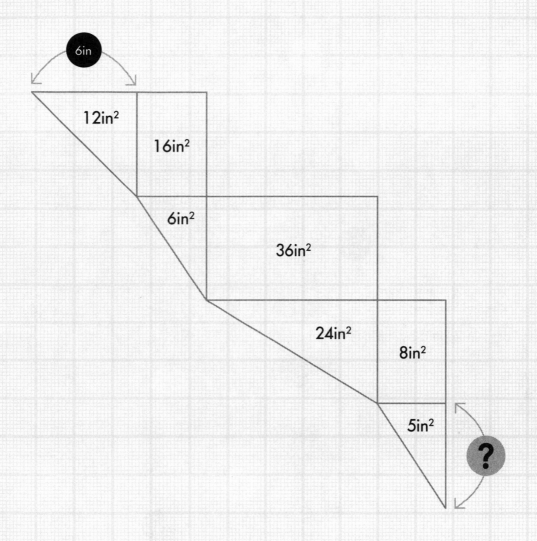

PUZZLE 8

Divide and rule! Sometimes it's helpful to make smaller shapes from larger ones. Find the length indicated by the question mark.

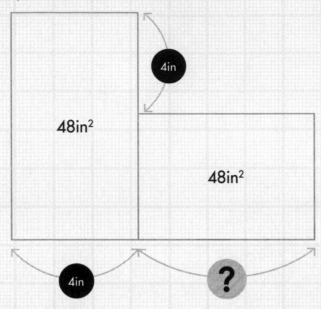

PUZZLE 9

Find the area indicated by the question mark.

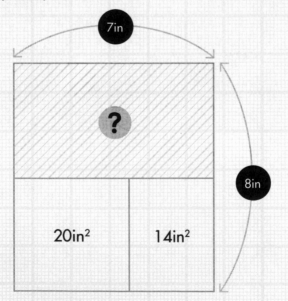

PUZZLE 10

Find the length indicated by the question mark.

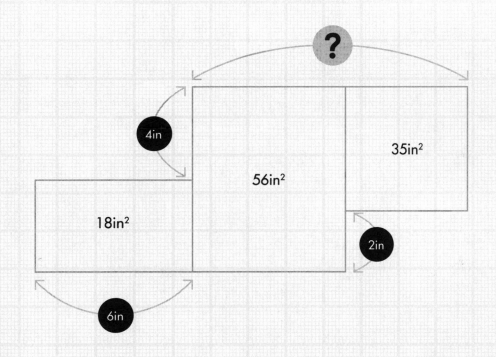

PUZZLE 11

Diagrams aren't necessarily drawn to scale.

Find the length indicated by the question mark.

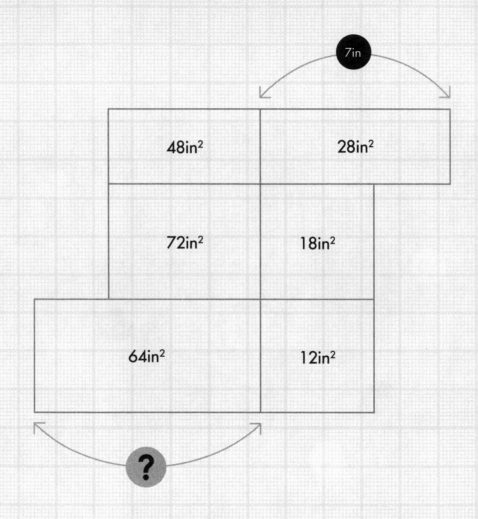

PUZZLE 12

Find the area indicated by the question mark.

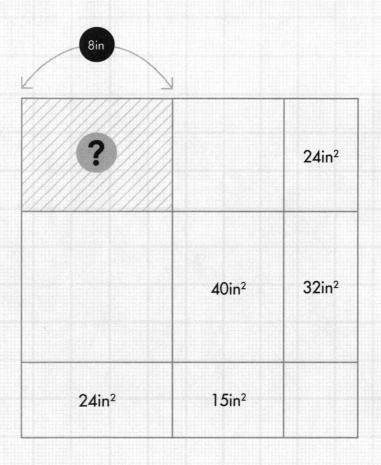

PUZZLE 13

Find the area indicated by the question mark.

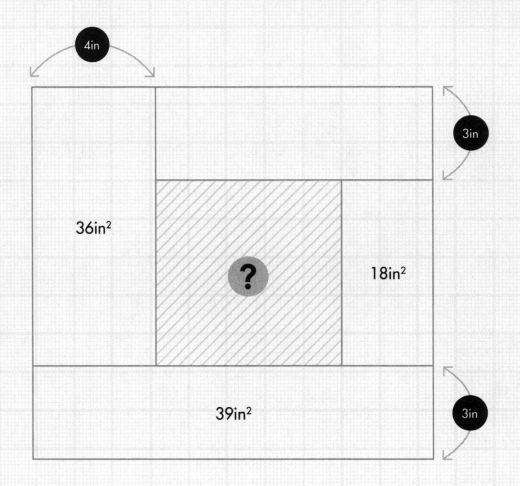

PUZZLE 14

Find the area indicated by the question mark.

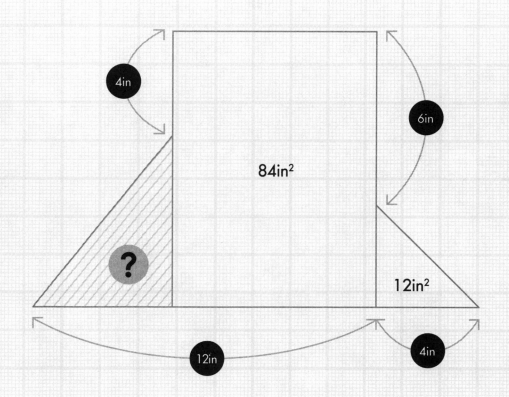

PUZZLE 15

Find the length indicated by the question mark.

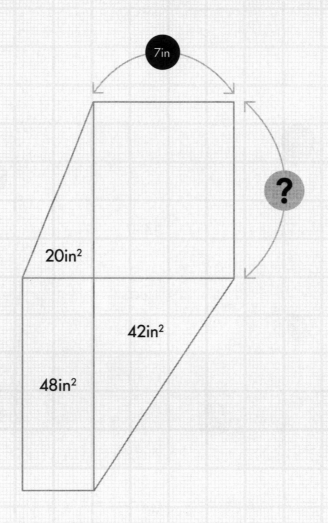

PUZZLE 16

Turn partial lengths into complete lengths.

Find the length indicated by the question mark.

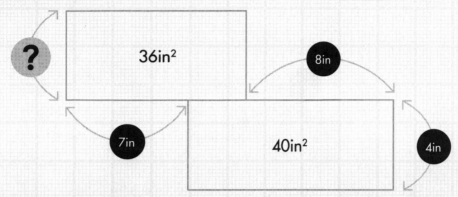

PUZZLE 17

Find the area indicated by the question mark.

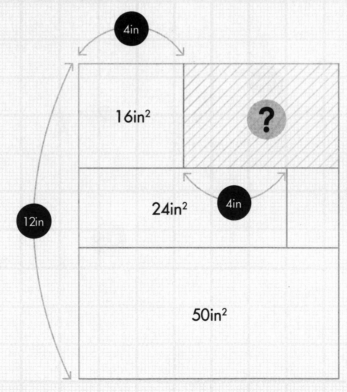

PUZZLE 18

Find the area indicated by the question mark.

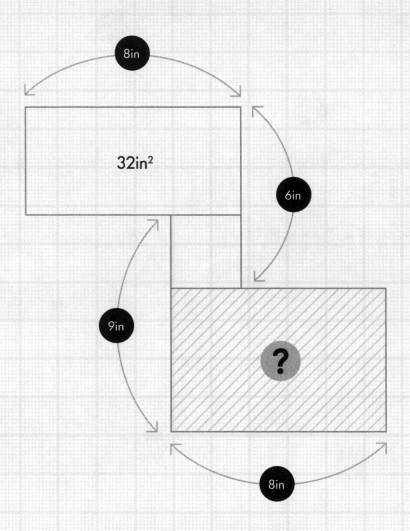

PUZZLE 19

Addition, subtraction, multiplication and division are all required. Find the area indicated by the question mark.

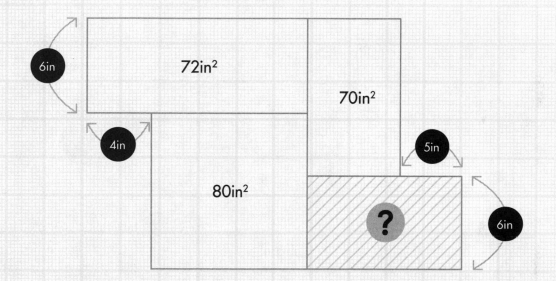

PUZZLE 20

The starting point isn't always given as a starter.
Find the area indicated by the question mark.

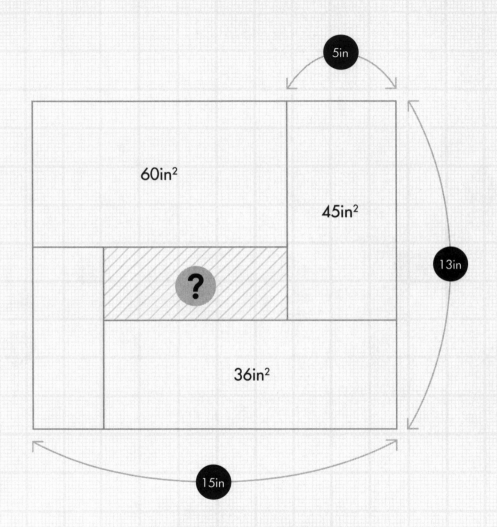

PUZZLE 21

Irregular shapes can comprise smaller regular shapes.
Find the area indicated by the question mark.

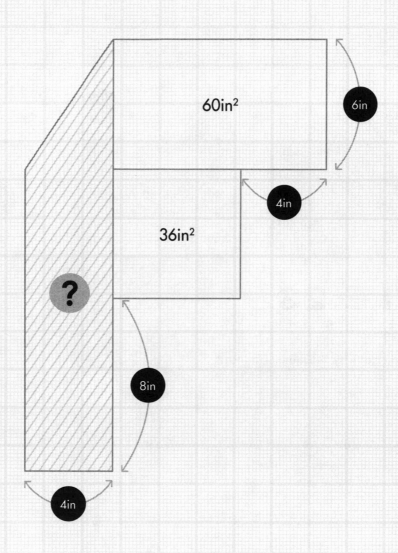

PUZZLE 22

Find the area indicated by the question mark.

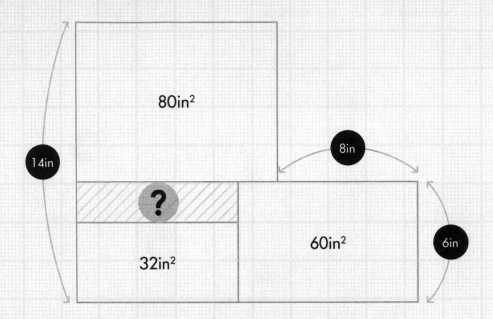

PUZZLE 23

Compare and contrast.

Find the area indicated by the question mark.

PUZZLE 24

Find the length indicated by the question mark.

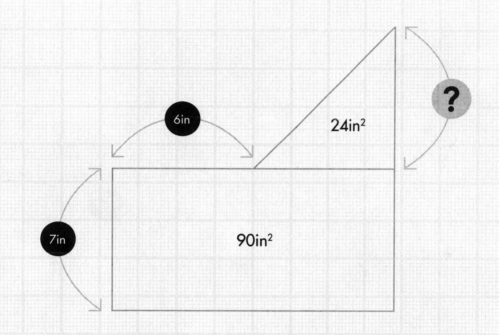

PUZZLE 25

Find the area indicated by the question mark.

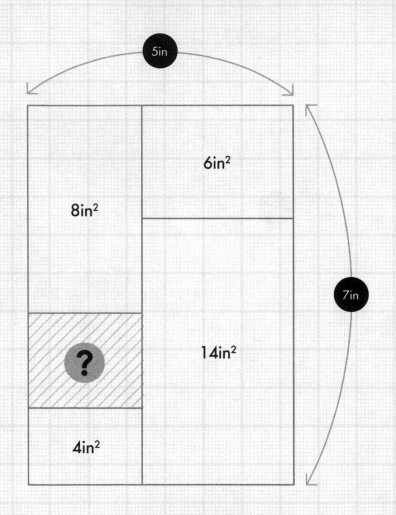

PUZZLE 26

Ratios. Find the length indicated by the question mark.

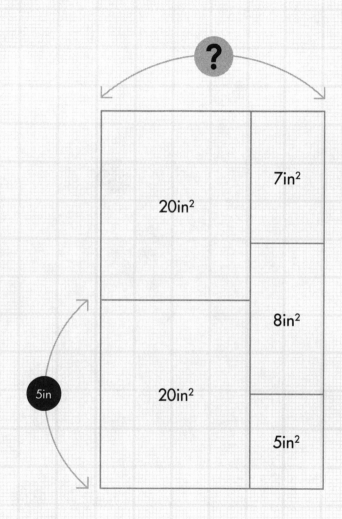

PUZZLE 27

Find the length indicated by the question mark.

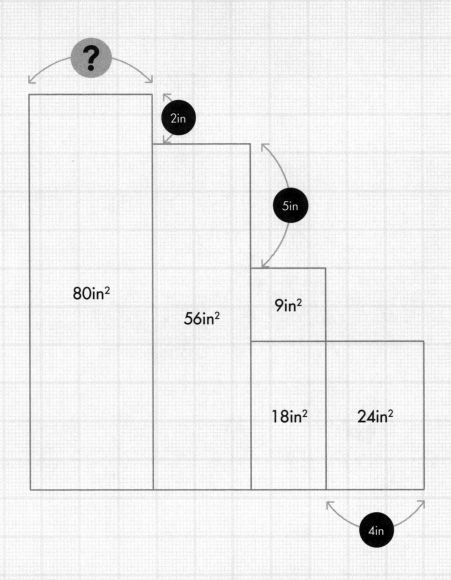

PUZZLE 28

Find the area indicated by the question mark.

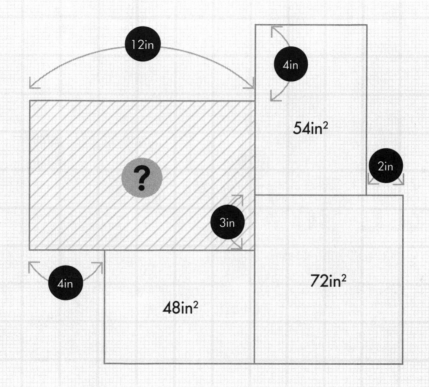

PUZZLE 29

Combine areas and compare.

Find the length indicated by the question mark.

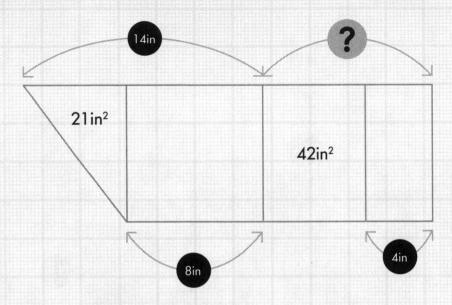

PUZZLE 30

Find the length indicated by the question mark.

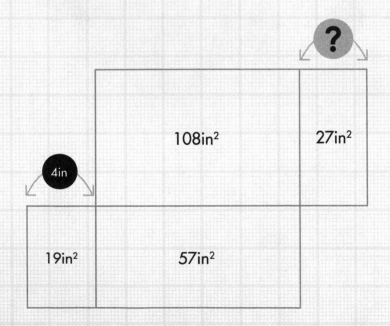

PUZZLE 31

Find the length indicated by the question mark.

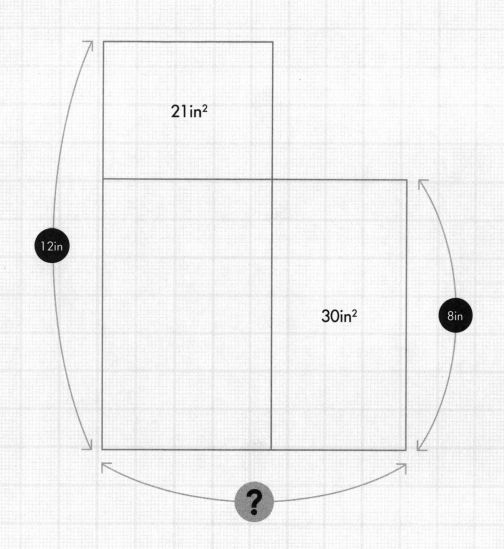

PUZZLE 32

Combine areas, bisect areas and compare values.

Find the area indicated by the question mark.

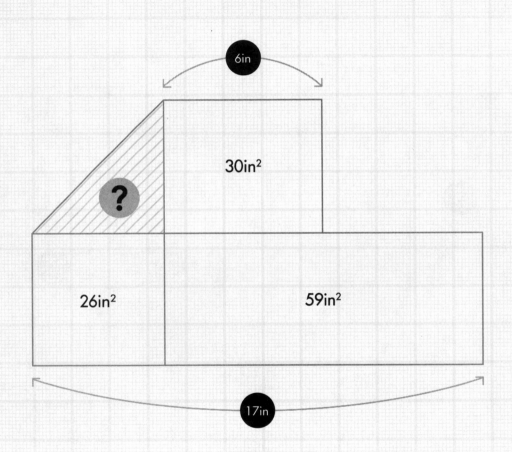

PUZZLE 33

Find the length indicated by the question mark.

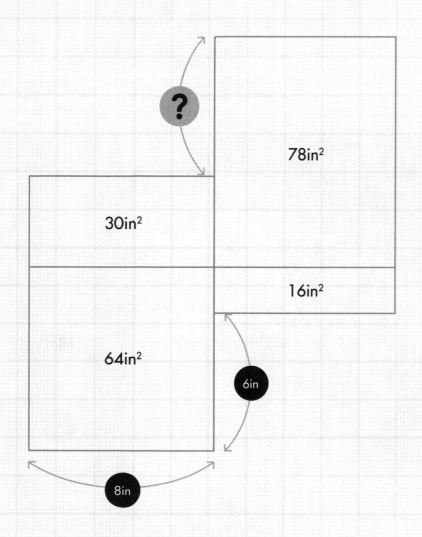

PUZZLE 34

Find the area indicated by the question mark.

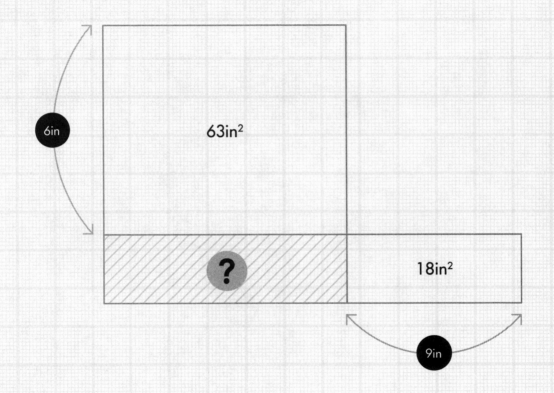

PUZZLE 35

Find the area indicated by the question mark.

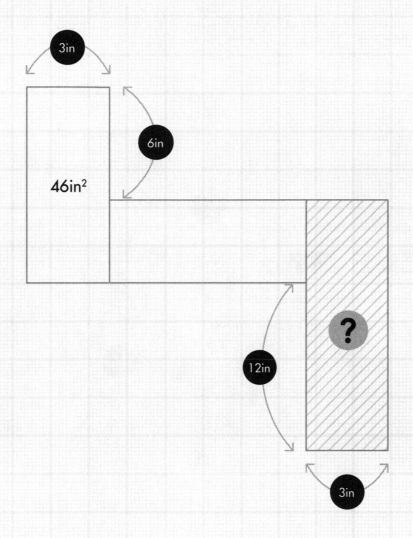

PUZZLE 36

Areas to combine aren't always adjacent.

Find the area indicated by the question mark.

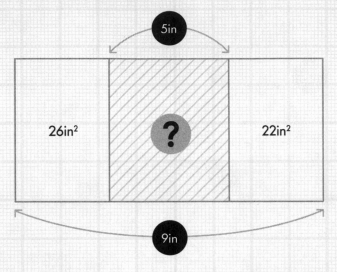

PUZZLE 37

Relative, rather than absolute, values can be the key.

Find the length indicated by the question mark.

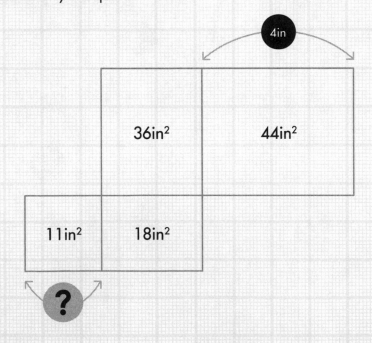

PUZZLE 38

Find the length indicated by the question mark.

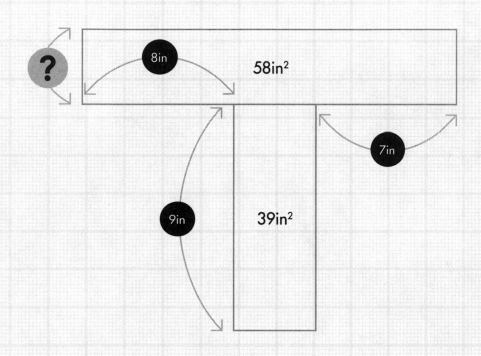

PUZZLE 39

Find the area indicated by the question mark.

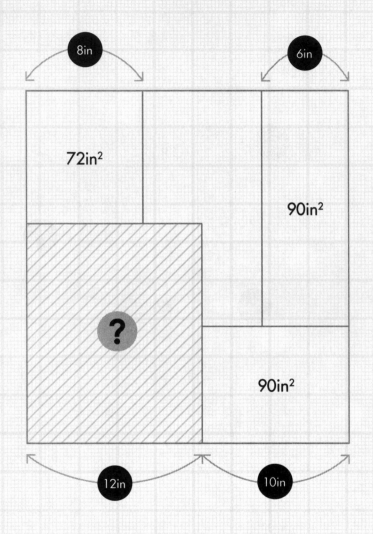

PUZZLE 40

Find the length indicated by the question mark.

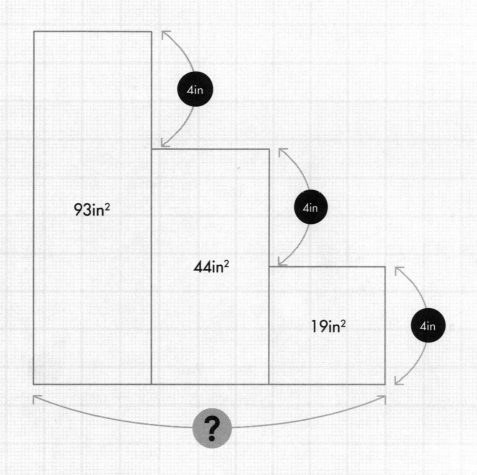

PUZZLE 41

Remember, sometimes it's relative.

Find the area indicated by the question mark.

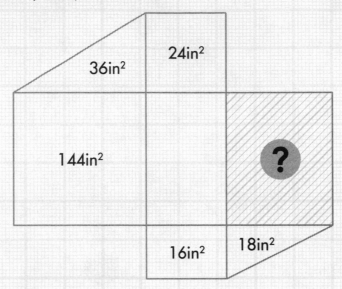

PUZZLE 42

Find the area indicated by the question mark.

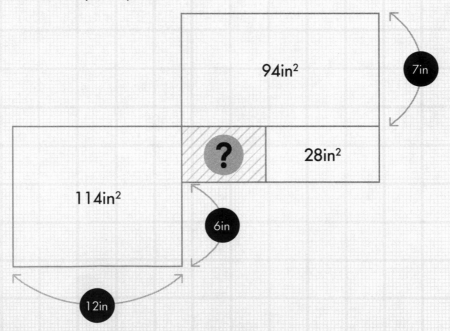

PUZZLE 43

Find the area indicated by the question mark.

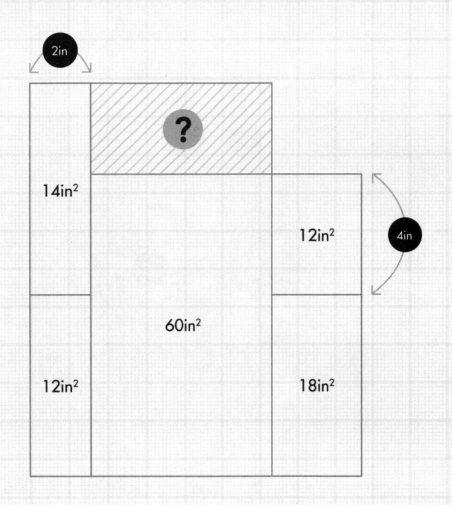

PUZZLE 44

Find the area indicated by the question mark.

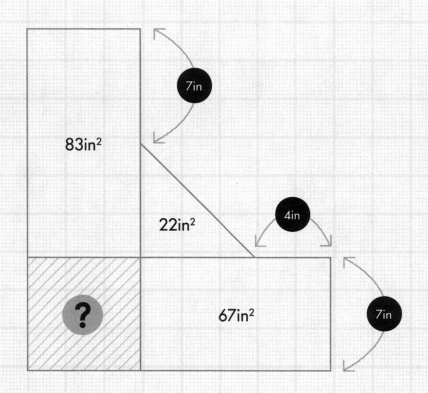

83in²

7in

22in²

4in

?

67in²

7in

PUZZLE 45

Irregular shapes can be divided into regular shapes.
Find the area indicated by the question mark.

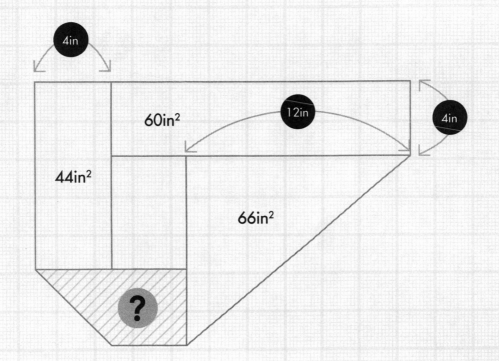

PUZZLE 46

Find the length indicated by the question mark.

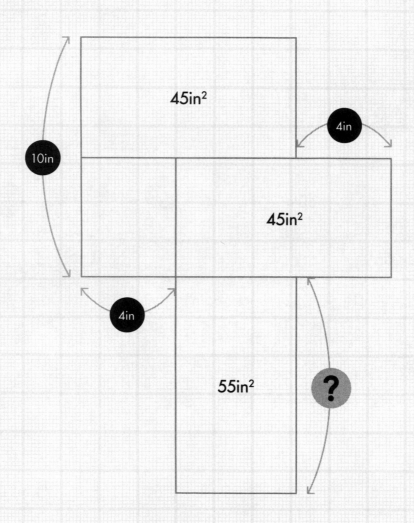

45in²

4in

10in

45in²

4in

55in²

?

PUZZLE 47

Find the area indicated by the question mark.

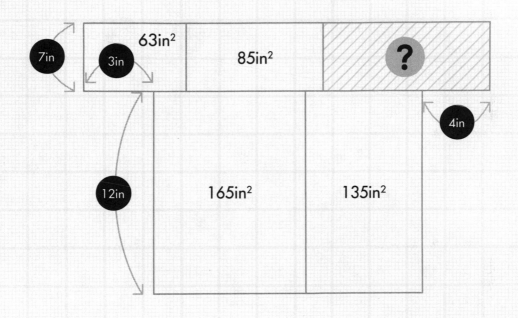

PUZZLE 48

The total area can be helpful.

Find the length indicated by the question mark.

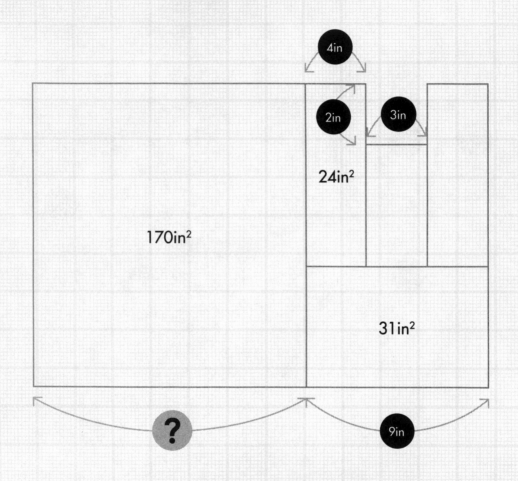

PUZZLE 49

Complete the full rectangle.

Find the length indicated by the question mark.

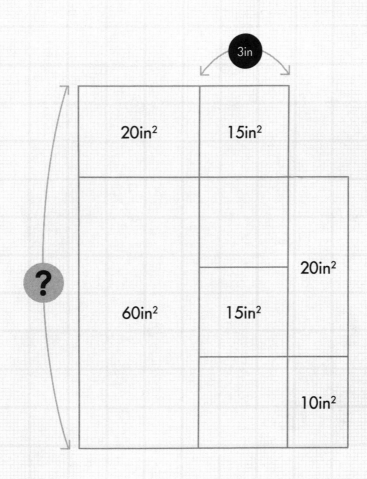

PUZZLE 50

Find the length indicated by the question mark.

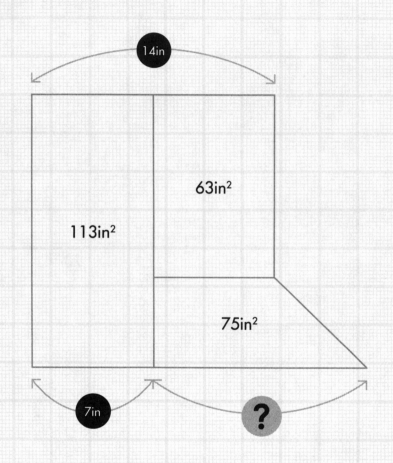

PUZZLE 51

Find the length indicated by the question mark.

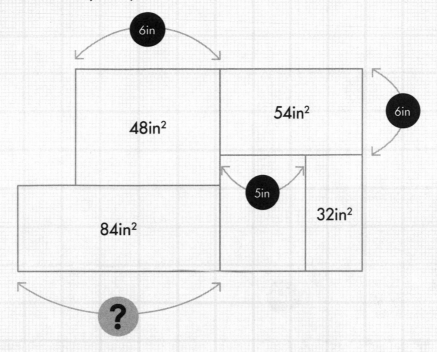

PUZZLE 52

The only way to proceed here is by creating the full rectangle. Find the area indicated by the question mark.

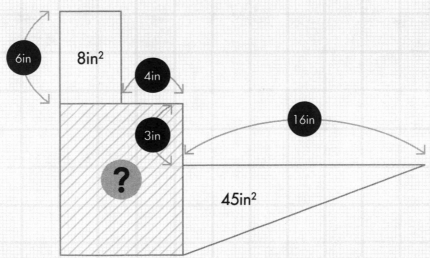

PUZZLE 53

Find the length indicated by the question mark.

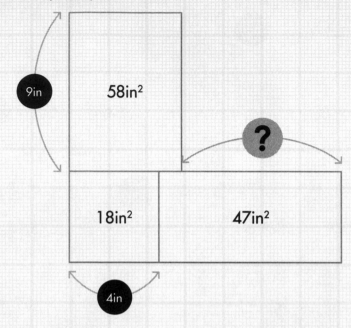

PUZZLE 54

Find the length indicated by the question mark.

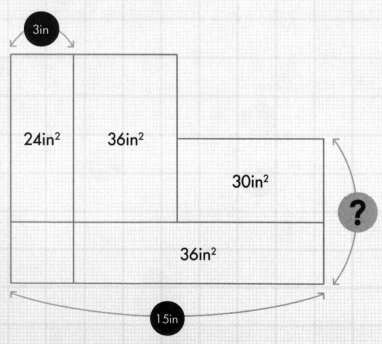

PUZZLE 55

Divide and divide again.

Find the area indicated by the question mark.

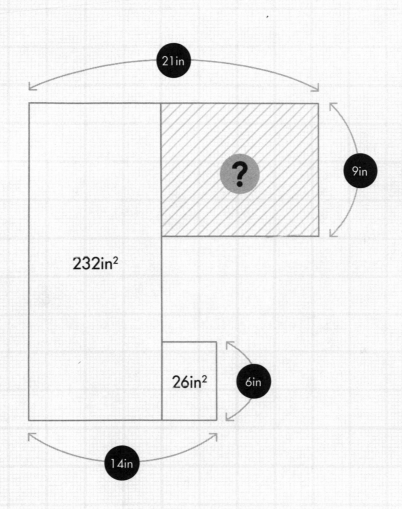

PUZZLE 56

Find the area indicated by the question mark.

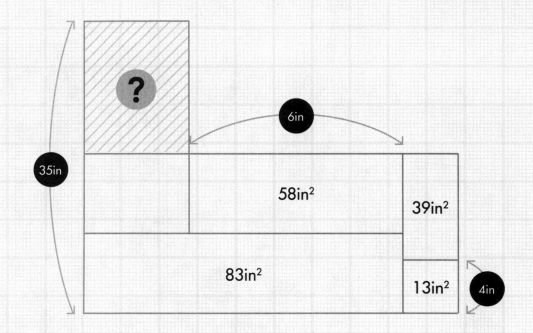

PUZZLE 57

Find the length indicated by the question mark.

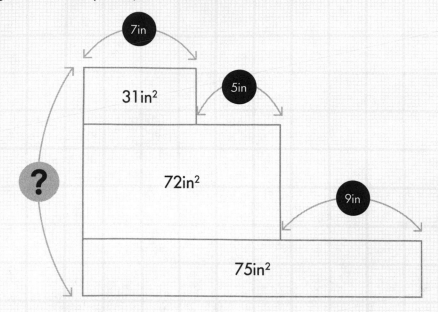

PUZZLE 58

Find the area indicated by the question mark.

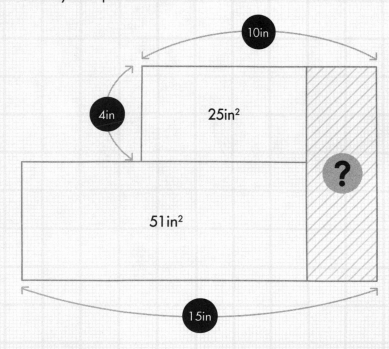

PUZZLE 59

Here, you may need to add more before you can take away. Find the area indicated by the question mark.

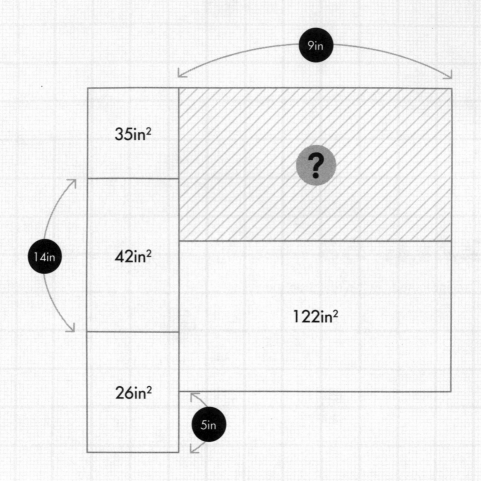

PUZZLE 60

Find the area indicated by the question mark.

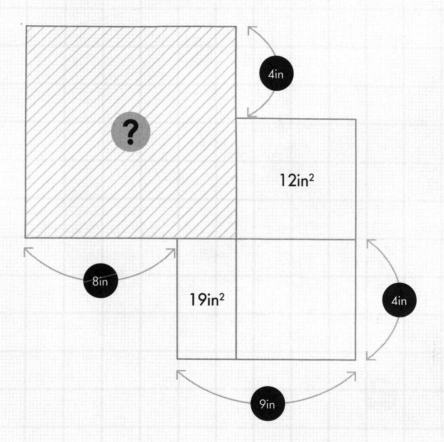

PUZZLE 61

Engage a number of strategies here and work round the grid. Find the length indicated by the question mark.

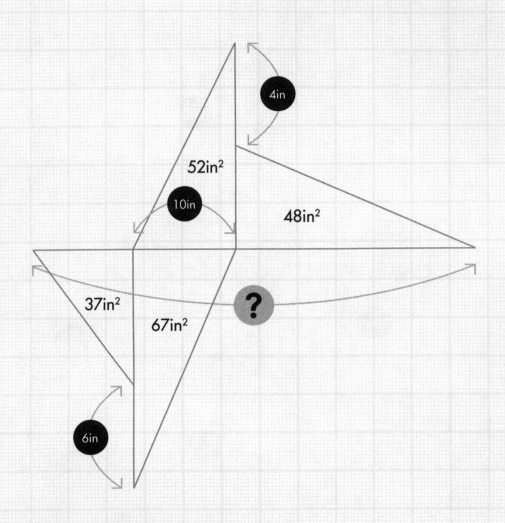

PUZZLE 62

Find the length indicated by the question mark.

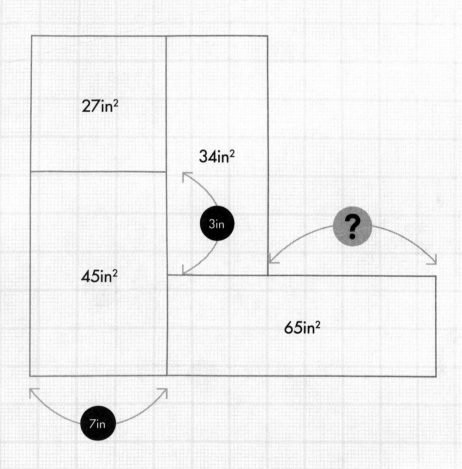

PUZZLE 63

Find the area indicated by the question mark.

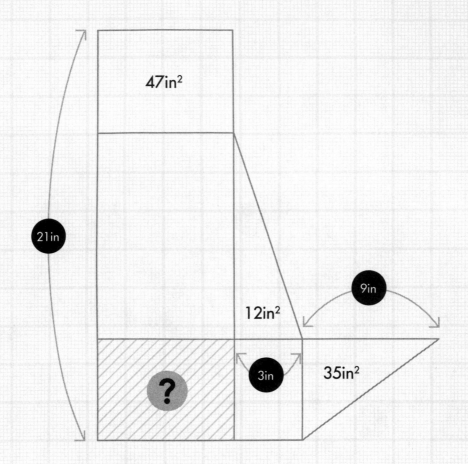

PUZZLE 64

Find the length indicated by the question mark.

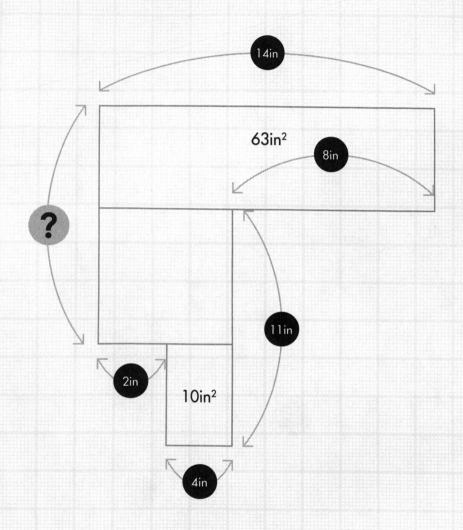

PUZZLE 65

Find the area indicated by the question mark.

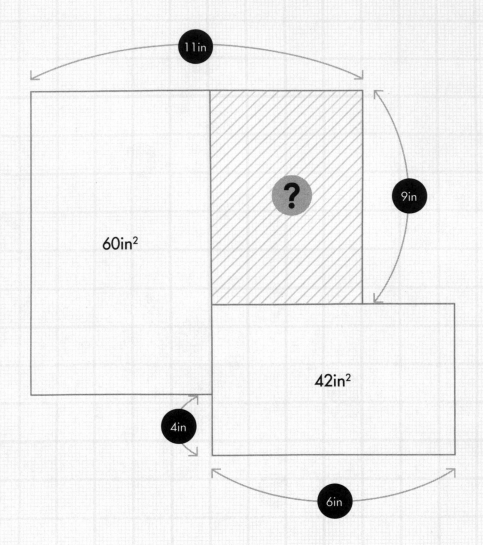

PUZZLE 66

Partial values can be revealing.

Find the area indicated by the question mark.

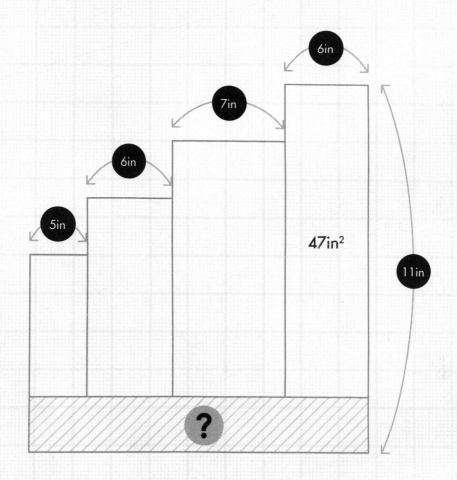

PUZZLE 67

Very tricky – remember the importance of relative values.

Find the length indicated by the question mark.

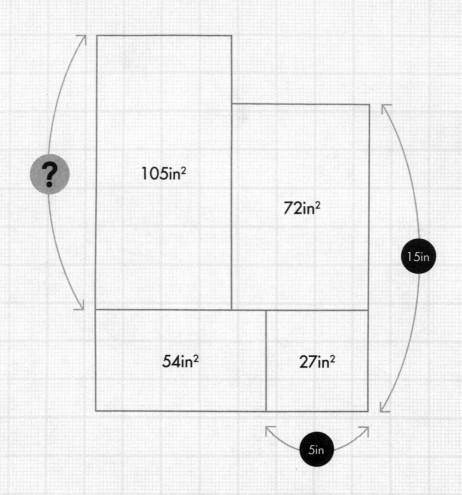

PUZZLE 68

Find the area indicated by the question mark.

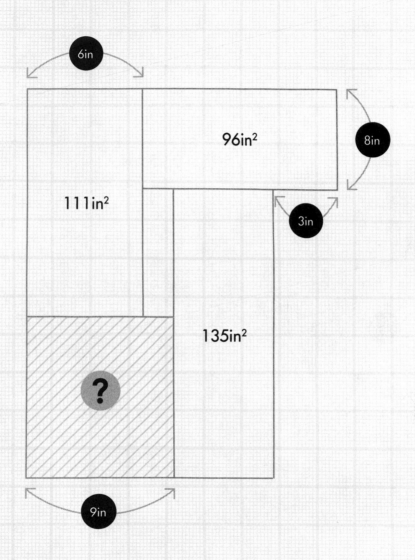

PUZZLE 69

Find the length indicated by the question mark.

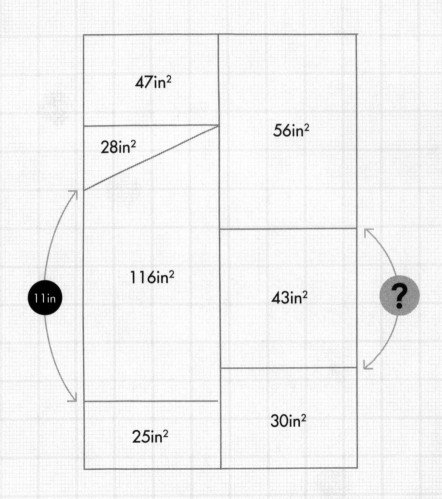

PUZZLE 70

Absolute values and relative values can be equally important. Find the length indicated by the question mark.

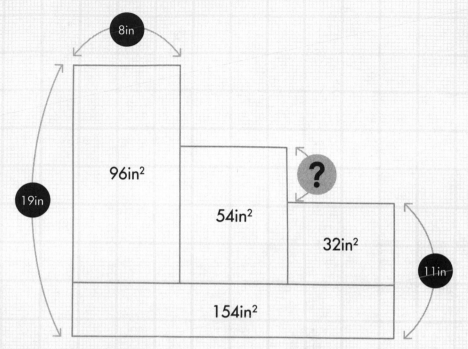

PUZZLE 71

Here's your first 3D puzzle.

Find the area indicated by the question mark.

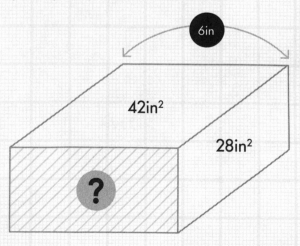

PUZZLE 72

Find the area indicated by the question mark.

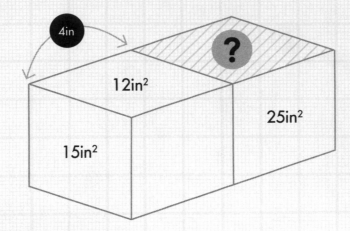

PUZZLE 73

Find the length indicated by the question mark.

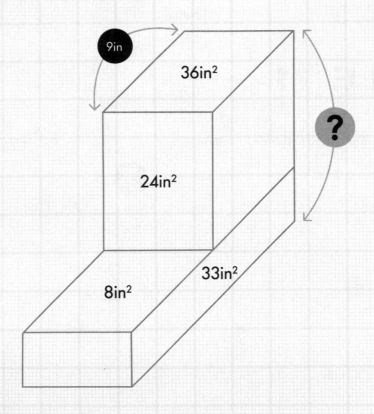

PUZZLE 74

Find the area indicated by the question mark.

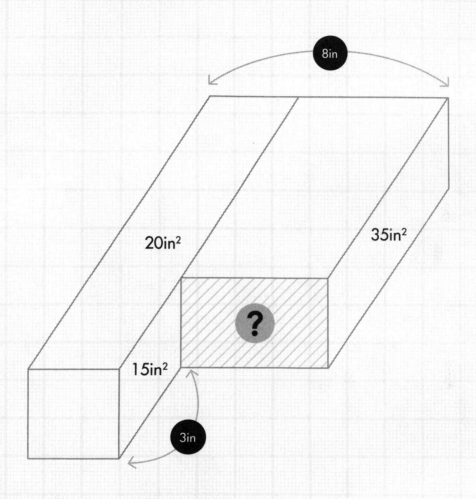

PUZZLE 75

Find the area indicated by the question mark.

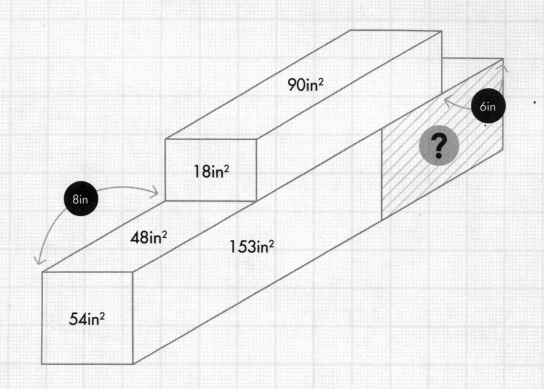

PUZZLE 76

Relative values can be just as important in 3D as in 2D.

Find the area indicated by the question mark.

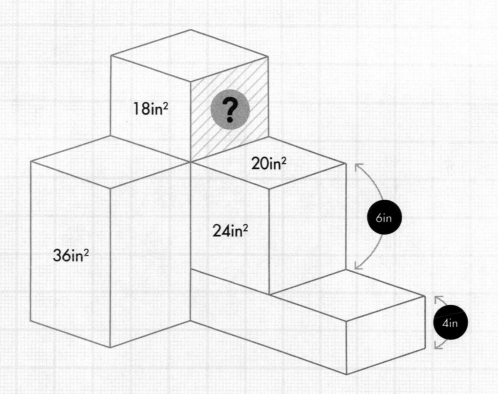

PUZZLE 77

Find the area indicated by the question mark.

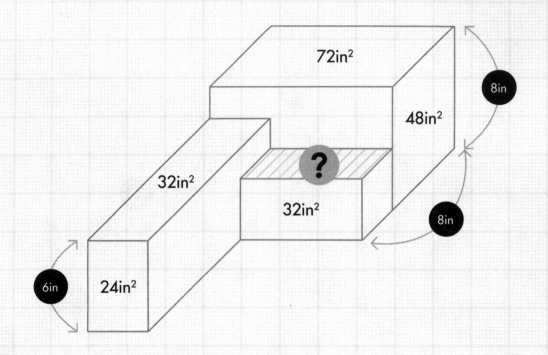

PUZZLE 78

Find the length indicated by the question mark.

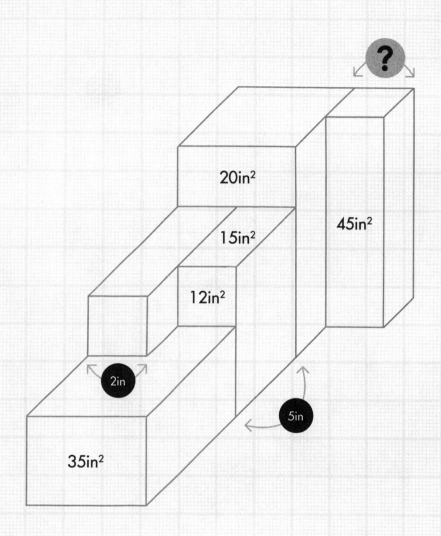

PUZZLE 79

Find the area indicated by the question mark.

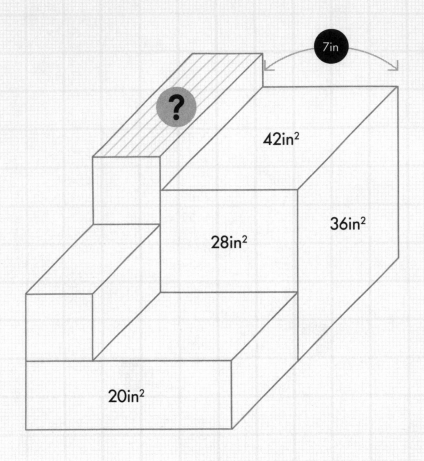

PUZZLE 80

Find the area indicated by the question mark.

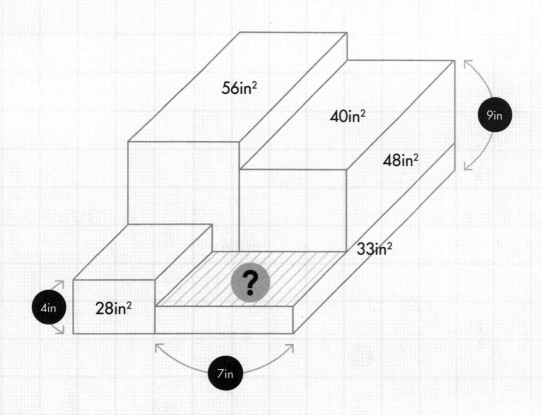

56in²

40in²

48in²

9in

33in²

?

4in

28in²

7in

AREA² MAZE SOLUTIONS

PUZZLE 1: 9in

? = 54in² ÷ 6in

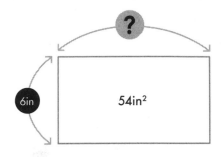

PUZZLE 2: 4in

Length A = 18in² ÷ 3in = 6in
? = 24in² ÷ 6in = 4in

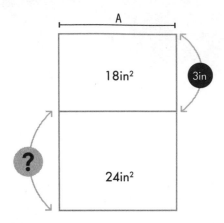

PUZZLE 3: 10in²

Length A = 20in² ÷ 4in = 5in
Length B = 12in² ÷ 3in = 4in
Create **triangle C**
The total area of **triangle C** and triangle **?** = 4in x 5in = 20in²
Therefore, **?** = 20in² ÷ 2 = 10in²

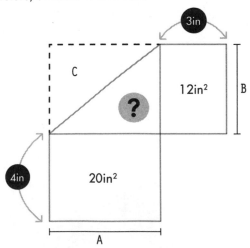

PUZZLE 4: 30in²

Length A = 8in – 5in = 3in
Length B = 18in² ÷ 3in = 6in
Therefore, **?** = 6in x 5in = 30in²

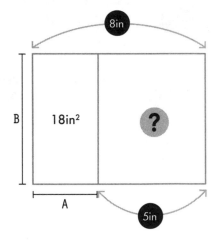

PUZZLE 5: 21in²

Length A = 9in² ÷ 3in = 3in
Length B = 15in² ÷ 3in = 5in
Length C = 35in² ÷ 5in = 7in
Therefore, **?** = 3in x 7in = 21in²

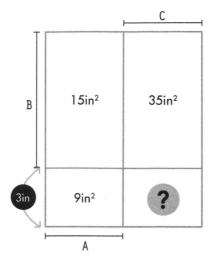

PUZZLE 6: 5in

Triangle A = 10in²
Triangle B = 15in²
Total area of **A** +10in² + 25in² + 15in² + **B** = 75in²
The rectangle with area 25in² = 75in² ÷ 3
Therefore **?** = 15in ÷ 3 = 5in

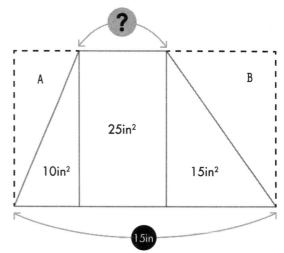

PUZZLE 7: 5in

Create **triangle A**
Triangle A = 12in²
Length B = 24in² ÷ 6in = 4in
Length C = 16in² ÷ 4in = 4in
Create **triangle D**
Triangle D = 6in²
Length E = 12in² ÷ 4in = 3in
Length F = 36in² ÷ 3in = 12in
Create **triangle G**
Triangle G = 24in²
Length H = 48in² ÷ 12in = 4in
Length I = 8in² ÷ 4in = 2in
Create **triangle J**
Triangle J + 5in² = 10in²
? = 10in² ÷ 2in = 5in

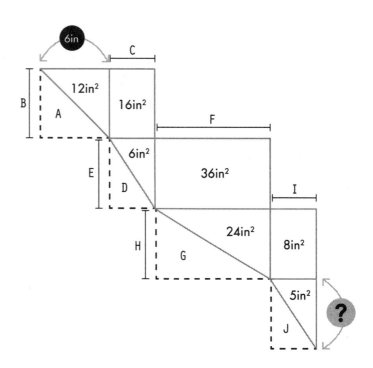

71

PUZZLE 8: 6in

Create **rectangles A** and **B**
Rectangle A = 4in x 4in = 16in²
Rectangle B = 48in² − 16in² = 32in²
Length C = 32in² ÷ 4in = 8in
? = 48in² ÷ 8in = 6in

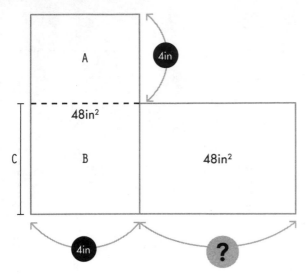

PUZZLE 9: 22in²

Total area = 7in x 8in = 56in²
? = 56in² − 20in² − 14in² = 22in²

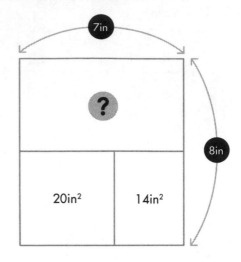

PUZZLE 10: 15in

Length A = 18in² ÷ 6in = 3in
Length B = 56in² ÷ (4in + 3in) = 8in
Length C = 4in + 3in − 2in = 5in
Length D = 35in² ÷ 5in = 7in
? = 8in + 7in = 15in

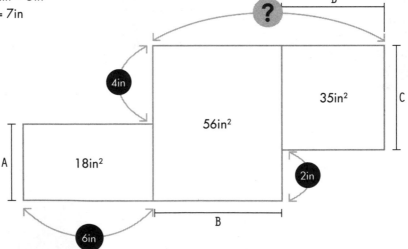

PUZZLE 11: 16in

Length A = $28in^2 \div 7in = 4in$
Length B = $48in^2 \div 4in = 12in$
Length C = $72in^2 \div 12in = 6in$
Length D = $18in^2 \div 6in = 3in$
Length E = $12in^2 \div 3in = 4in$
? = $64in^2 \div 4in = 16in$

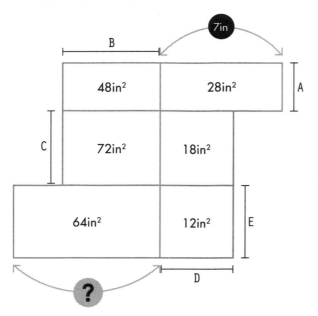

PUZZLE 12: 48in²

Length A = $24in^2 \div 8in = 3in$
Length B = $15in^2 \div 3in = 5in$
Length C = $40in^2 \div 5in = 8in$
Length D = $32in^2 \div 8in = 4in$
Length E = $24in^2 \div 4in = 6in$
? = $6in \times 8in = 48in^2$

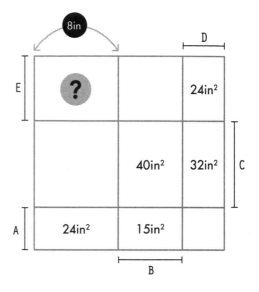

PUZZLE 13: 36in²

Length A = $36in^2 \div 4in = 9in$
Length B = $9in - 3in = 6in$
Length C = $39in^2 \div 3in = 13in$
Length D = $13in - 4in = 9in$
Length E = $18in^2 \div 6in = 3in$
Length F = $9in - 3in = 6in$
? = $6in \times 6in = 36in^2$

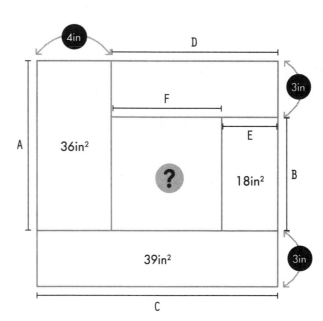

PUZZLE 14: 20in²

Create **triangle A**

Triangle A + 12in² = 24in²

Length B = 24in² ÷ 4in = 6in

Length C = 6in + 6in − 4in = 8in

Length D = 84in² ÷ (6in + 6in) = 7in

Length E = 12in − 7in = 5in

Create **triangle F**

Triangle F + area **?** = 8in x 5in = 40in²

? = 40in² ÷ 2 = 20in²

PUZZLE 15: 10in

Create **triangle A**

A + 42in² = 84in²

Length B = 84in² ÷ 7in = 12in

Length C = 48in² ÷ 12in = 4in

Create **triangle D**

D + 20in² = 40in²

? = 40in² ÷ 4in = 10in

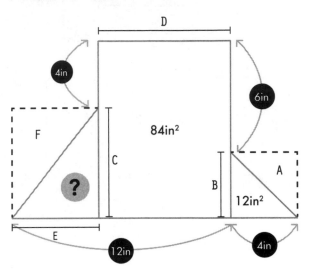

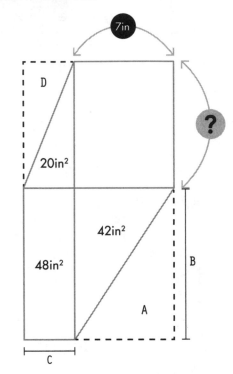

PUZZLE 16: 4in

Length A = 40in² ÷ 4in = 10in

Length B = 10in − 8in = 2in

? = 36in² ÷ (7in + 2in) = 4in

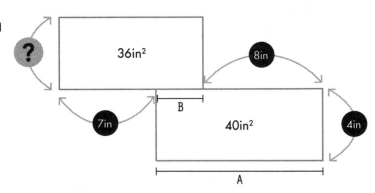

PUZZLE 17: 24in²

Length A = 16in² ÷ 4in = 4in
Length B = 24in² ÷ (4in + 4in) = 3in
Length C = 12in − 4in − 3in = 5in
Length D = 50in² ÷ 5in = 10in
Length E = 10in − 4in = 6in
? = 4in x 6in = 24in²

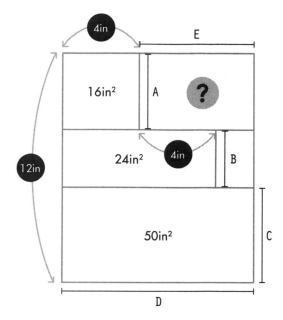

PUZZLE 18: 56in²

Length A = 32in² ÷ 8in = 4in
Length B = 6in − 4in = 2in
Length C = 9in − 2in = 7in
? = 7in x 8in = 56in²

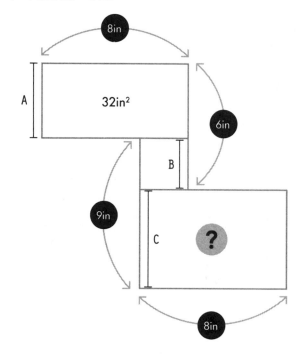

PUZZLE 19: 72in²

Length A = 72in² ÷ 6in = 12in
Length B = 12in − 4in = 8in
Length C = 80in² ÷ 8in = 10in
Length D = 10in − 6in = 4in
Length E = 6in + 4in = 10in
Length F = 70in² ÷ 10in = 7in
Length G = 7in + 5in = 12in
? = 12in x 6in = 72in²

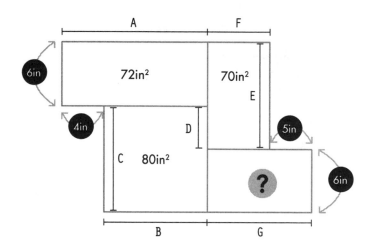

PUZZLE 20: 12in²

Length A = 15in − 5in = 10in
Length B = 60in² ÷ 10in = 6in
Length C = 45in² ÷ 5in = 9in
Length D = 13in − 9in = 4in
Length E = 36in² ÷ 4in = 9in
Length F = 15in − 9in = 6in
Length G = 13in − 6in = 7in
Length H = 10in − 6in = 4in
Length I = 7in − 4in = 3in
? = 4in x 3in = 12in²

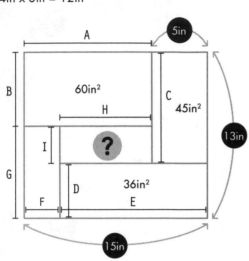

PUZZLE 21: 68in²

Length A = 60in² ÷ 6in = 10in
Length B = 10in − 4in = 6in
Length C = 36in² ÷ 6in = 6in
Create **rectangle D** and **triangle F**
D = 4in x (8in + 6in) = 56in²
Create **rectangle E**
E = 6in x 4in = 24in²
F = 24in² ÷ 2 = 12in²
? = 56in² + 12in² = 68in²

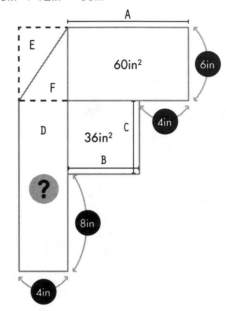

PUZZLE 22: 16in²

Create **rectangles A** and **B**
A = 8in x 6in = 48in²
B = 60in² − 48in² = 12in²
Length C = 12in² ÷ 6in = 2in
Length D = 14in − 6in = 8in
Create **rectangles E** and **F**
E = 2in x 8in = 16in²
F = 80in² − 16in² = 64in²
64in² = 16in² x 4
G = 2in x 4 = 8in
F + ? + 32in² = 14in x 8in = 112in²
? = 112in² − 64in² − 32in² = 16in²

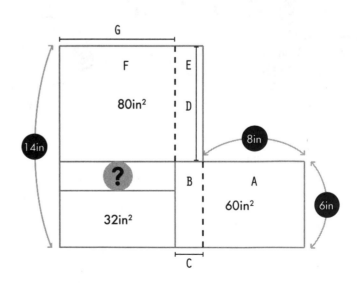

PUZZLE 23: 36in²

$27in^2 = 9in^2 \times 3$
$? = 12in^2 \times 3 = 36in^2$

9in²	27in²
12in²	**?**

PUZZLE 24: 7in

Create **rectangles A** and **B**
$A = 6in \times 7in = 42in^2$
$B = 90in^2 - 42in^2 = 48in^2$
Create **triangle C**
$C + 24in^2 = 48in^2 = B$
$? = 7in$

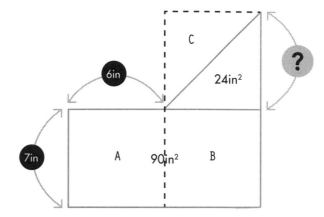

PUZZLE 25: 3in²

Total area $= 5in \times 7in = 35in^2$
$? = 35in^2 - 8in^2 - 6in^2 - 14in^2 - 4in^2 = 3in^2$

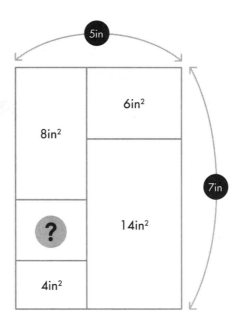

PUZZLE 26: 6in

Both rectangles of 20in² have the same width, so length
A = 5in
Total area = 20in² + 20in² + 7in² + 8in² + 5in² = 60in²
? = 60in² ÷ (5in + 5in) = 6in

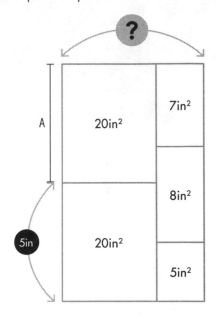

PUZZLE 27: 5in

Length A = 24in² ÷ 4in = 6in
Length B = 18in² ÷ 6in = 3in
Length C = 9in² ÷ 3in = 3in
Length D = 6in + 3in + 5in + 2in = 16in²
? = 80in² ÷ 16in = 5in

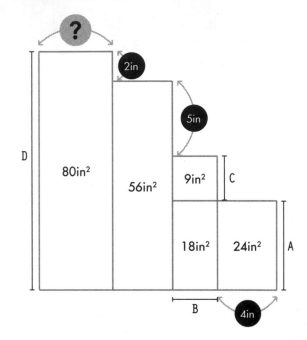

PUZZLE 28: 96in²

Length A = 12in − 4in = 8in
Length B = 48in² ÷ 8in = 6in
Length C = 6in + 3in = 9in
Length D = 72in² ÷ 9in = 8in
Length E = 8in − 2in = 6in
Length F = 54in² ÷ 6in = 9in
Length G = 9in − 4in = 5in
? = 12in x (5in + 3in) = 96in²

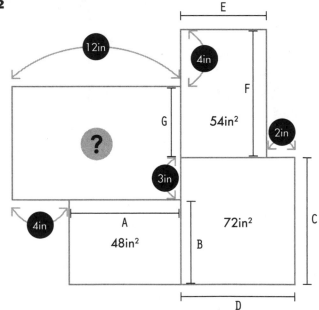

PUZZLE 29: 10in

Create **triangle A**
$A + 21in^2 = 42in^2$
Length B = Length C
? = $14in - 8in + 4in = 10in$

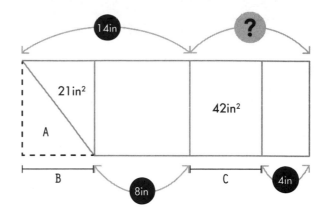

PUZZLE 30: 3in

$57in^2 = 19in^2 \times 3$
Length A = $4in \times 3 = 12in$
$108in^2 = 27in^2 \times 4$
? = $12in \div 4 = 3in$

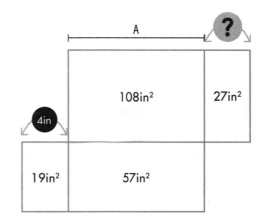

PUZZLE 31: 9in

Length A = $12in - 8in = 4in$
$4in = 8in \div 2$
B = $21in^2 \times 2 = 42in^2$
$B + 30in^2 = 72in^2$
? = $72in^2 \div 8in = 9in$

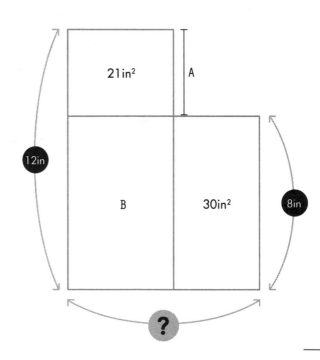

PUZZLE 32: 13in²

Length A = 30in² ÷ 6in = 5in
Length B = 26in² + 59in² ÷ 17in = 5in
Create **triangle C**
Length A = Length B
C + ? = 26in²
? = 26in² ÷ 2 = 13in²

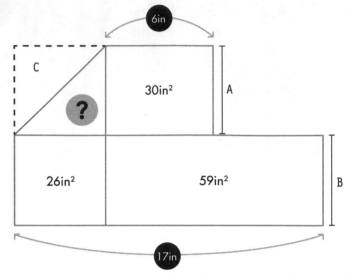

PUZZLE 33: 6in

Length A = 64in² ÷ 8in = 8in
Length B = 8in − 6in = 2in
Length C = 16in² ÷ 2in = 8in
Create **rectangles D** and **E**
As **length C** = 8in, **area D** = 30in²
E = 78in² − 30in² = 48in²
? = 48in² ÷ 8in = 6in

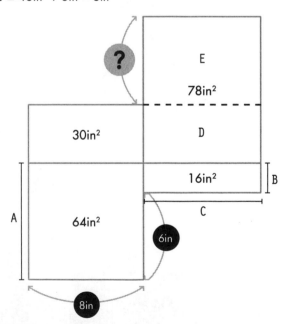

PUZZLE 34: 21in²

Create **rectangle A**
A = 9in x 6in = 54in²
54in² = 18in² x 3
63in² = **?** x 3
? = 21in²

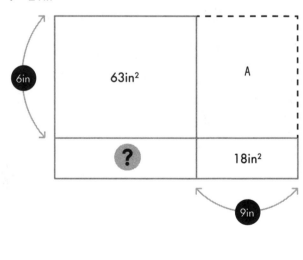

PUZZLE 35: 64in²

Create **rectangles A** and **B**
$A = 3in \times 6in = 18in^2$
$B = 46in^2 - 18in^2 = 28in^2$
Create **rectangles C** and **D**
$B = C = 28in^2$
$D = 12in \times 3in = 36in^2$
$? = 28in^2 + 36in^2 = 64in^2$

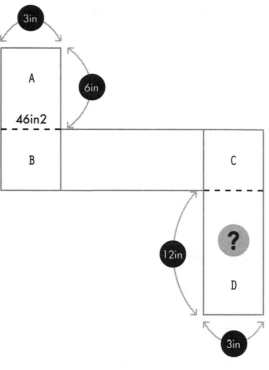

PUZZLE 36: 60in²

Rectangles A + B = $48in^2$
Length C + Length D = $9in - 5in = 4in$
Length E = $48in^2 \div 4in = 12in$
$? = 12in \times 5in = 60in^2$

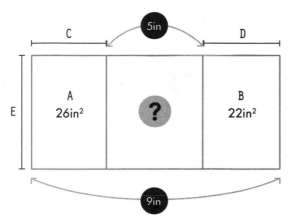

PUZZLE 37: 2in

Create **rectangle A**
$18in^2 = 36in^2 \div 2$
$A = 44in^2 \div 2 = 22in^2$
$22in^2 \div 2 = 11in^2$
$? = 4in \div 2 = 2in$

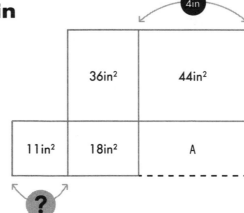

PUZZLE 38: 3in

Create **rectangles A** and **B**
$A = 9in \times 8in = 72in^2$
$B = 7in \times 9in = 63in^2$
$72in^2 + 39in^2 + 63in^2 = 174in^2$
$58in^2 = 174in^2 \div 3$
$? = 9in \div 3 = 3in$

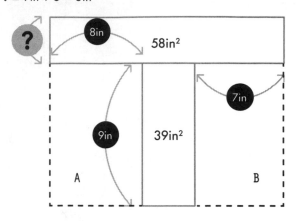

PUZZLE 39: 180in²

Length A $= 72in^2 \div 8in = 9in$
Length B $= 90in^2 \div 10in = 9in$
Length C = **length D**
$12in = 6in \times 2$
$? = 90in^2 \times 2 = 180in^2$

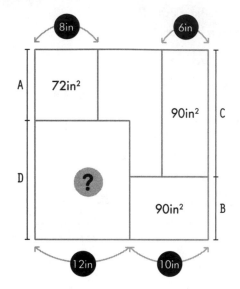

PUZZLE 40: 18in

Create **rectangles A** and **B**
A and **B** have the same height.
$A = 44in^2 \div 2 = 22in^2$
$B = 22in^2$
Create **rectangles C** and **D**
C is twice as high as **D**
Rectangle C = **rectangle D** $\times 2$
$D = 93in^2 \div 3 = 31in^2$
$D + B + 19in^2 = 72in^2$
$72in^2 \div 4in = 18in$

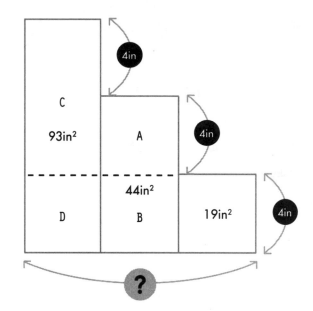

PUZZLE 41: 108in²

Create **triangle A** = 36in²
36in² + 36in² = 72in²
72in² = 144in² ÷ 2
The **central rectangle** therefore
= 24in² x 2 = 48in²
48in² = 16in² x 3
Create **triangle B** = 18in²
18in² + 18in² = 36in²
? = 36in² x 3 = 108in²

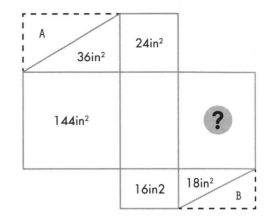

PUZZLE 42: 19in²

Create **rectangles A** and **B**
A = 6in x 12in = 72in²
B = 114in² – 72 in² = 42in²
Rectangle B has an area 50% greater than 28in², so
12in is 50% greater than **length C** = 8in
Create **rectangles D** and **E**
Rectangle D = 7in x 8in = 56in²
Rectangle E = 94in² – 56in² = 38in²
D = 28in² x 2, so **E** = **?** x 2
? = 38in² ÷ 2 = 19in²

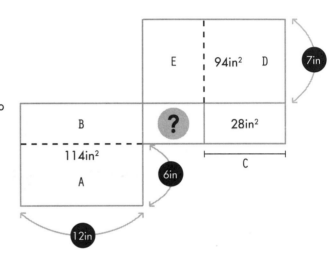

PUZZLE 43: 18in²

Length A = 12in² ÷ 4in = 3in
Length B = 18in² ÷ 3in = 6in
Length C = 60in² ÷ (4in + 6in) = 6in
Length D = 12in² ÷ 2in = 6in
Length E = 14in² ÷ 2in = 7in
Length F = (6in + 7in) – (6in + 4in) = 3in
? = 6in x 3in = 18in²

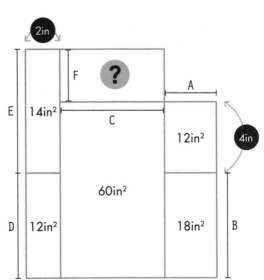

PUZZLE 44: 39in²

Create **rectangles A** and **B**
$A = 7\text{in} \times 4\text{in} = 28\text{in}^2$
Rectangle B = $67\text{in}^2 - 28\text{in}^2 = 39\text{in}^2$
Create **triangle C** = 22in^2
Create **rectangle D**
Rectangle D is the same height and width as **rectangle B** = 39in^2
Rectangle D + **triangle C** + $22\text{in}^2 = 83\text{in}^2$
Therefore **?** = **rectangle B** = 39in^2

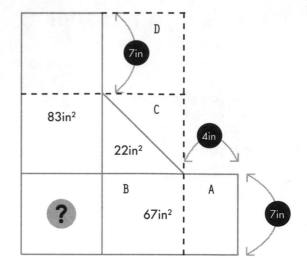

PUZZLE 45: 20in²

Create **triangle A** = 66in^2
Length B = $(66\text{in}^2 + 66\text{in}^2) \div 12\text{in} = 11\text{in}$
Length C = $44\text{in}^2 \div 4\text{in} = 11\text{in}$
Create **triangles D** and **E**
Length F = $15\text{in} - 11\text{in} = 4\text{in}$
Triangles D and **E** together = $4\text{in} \times 4\text{in} = 16\text{in}^2$
Triangle E = $16\text{in}^2 \div 2 = 8\text{in}^2$
Create **rectangles G** and **H**
$G = 12\text{in} \times 4\text{in} = 48\text{in}^2$
$H = 60\text{in}^2 - 48\text{in}^2 = 12\text{in}^2$
Length I = $12\text{in}^2 \div 4\text{in} = 3\text{in}$
Rectangle J = $3\text{in} \times 4\text{in} = 12\text{in}^2$
? = $8\text{in}^2 + 12\text{in}^2 = 20\text{in}^2$

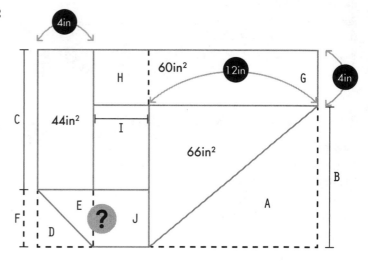

PUZZLE 46: 11in

Create **rectangles A** and **B**
Rectangle A = rectangle C
Rectangles A + B = rectangles B + C = 45in^2
Length D = (45in^2 + 45in^2) ÷ 10in = 9in
Length E = 9in − 4in = 5in
? = 55in^2 ÷ 5in = 11in

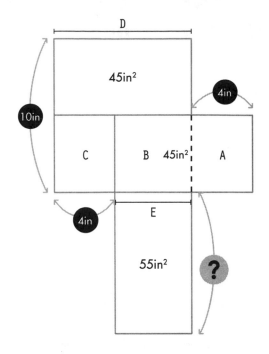

PUZZLE 47: 76in^2

Length A = (165in^2 + 135in^2) ÷ 12in = 25in
Length B = 3in + 25in + 4in = 32in
? + 85in^2 + 63in^2 = 7in x 32in = 224in^2
? = 224in^2 − 85in^2 − 63in^2 = 76in^2

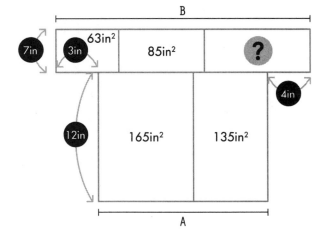

PUZZLE 48: 18in

Length A = $(24\text{in}^2 \div 4\text{in}) - 2\text{in} = 4\text{in}$
Rectangle B = $4\text{in} \times 3\text{in} = 12\text{in}^2$
Create **rectangle C** = $2\text{in} \times 3\text{in} = 6\text{in}^2$
Length D = $9\text{in} - 4\text{in} - 3\text{in} = 2\text{in}$
Rectangle E = $2\text{in} \times 6\text{in} = 12\text{in}^2$
$24\text{in}^2 + 31\text{in}^2 + \textbf{B} + \textbf{C} + \textbf{E} = 85\text{in}^2$
$85\text{in}^2 \times 2 = 170\text{in}^2$
? = $9\text{in} \times 2 = 18\text{in}$

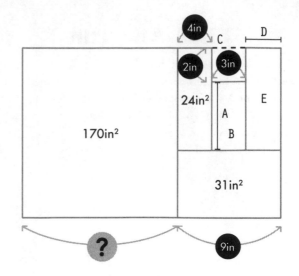

PUZZLE 49: 20in

Create **rectangle A**
$20\text{in}^2 = 60\text{in}^2 \div 3$, so **rectangle A** = $20\text{in}^2 + 10\text{in}^2 \div 3 = 10\text{in}^2$
$\textbf{B} + 15\text{in}^2 + \textbf{C} = 15\text{in}^2 \times 3 = 45\text{in}^2$
$15\text{in}^2 + 45\text{in}^2 = 60\text{in}^2$
? = $60\text{in}^2 \div 3\text{in} = 20\text{in}$

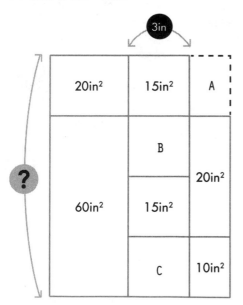

PUZZLE 50: 14in

Length A = $14\text{in} - 7\text{in} = 7\text{in}$
Length B = $63\text{in}^2 \div 7\text{in} = 9\text{in}$
Create **rectangles C** and **D**
Rectangle C = $7\text{in} \times 9\text{in} = 63\text{in}^2$
Rectangle D = $113\text{in}^2 - 63\text{in}^2 = 50\text{in}^2$
Create **rectangle E** and **triangle F**
E = D = 50in^2
Triangle F = $75\text{in}^2 - 50\text{in}^2 = 25\text{in}^2$
Create **triangle G = triangle F**
$\textbf{E} + \textbf{F} + \textbf{G} = \textbf{D} \times 2$
? = $7\text{in} \times 2 = 14\text{in}$

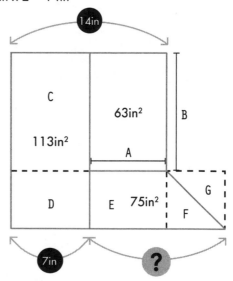

PUZZLE 51: 14in

Length **A** = 54in² ÷ 6in = 9in
Length **B** = 9in − 5in = 4in
Length **C** = 32in² ÷ 4in = 8in
Length **D** = 48in² ÷ 6in = 8in
Length **E** = 6in + **C** − **D** = 6in
? = 84in² ÷ 6in = 14in

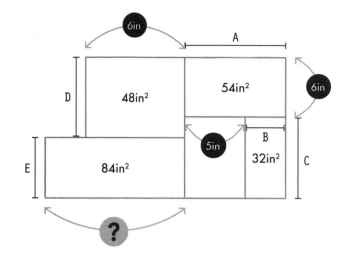

PUZZLE 52: 46in²

Create **rectangle A** = 6in x 4in = 24in²
Create **rectangles B** and **C**
B = 6in x 16in = 96in²
C = 3in x 16in = 48in²
Create **triangle D** = 45in²
B = (**A** + 8in²) x 3
? = (**C** + 45in² + **D**) ÷ 3 = 46in²

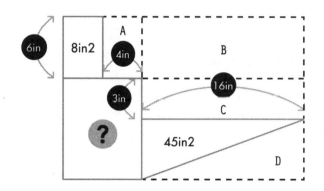

PUZZLE 53: 8in

Create **rectangles A** and **B**
A = 9in x 4in = 36in²
B = 58in² − 36in² = 22in²
Create **rectangles C** and **D**
A = 18in² x 2
C = **B** ÷ 2 = 11in²
D = 47in² − 11in² = 36in²
36in² = 18in² x 2, so **?** = 4in x 2 = 8in

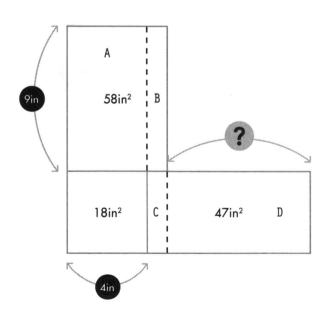

PUZZLE 54: 7in

Length A = $24in^2 \div 3in = 8in$
Length B = $15in - 3in = 12in$
Create **rectangle C**
C = $(12in \times 8in) - 36in^2 - 30in^2 = 30in^2$
Create **rectangles D** and **E**
As **C** = $30in^2$, so **D** = **E** = $36in^2 \div 2 = 18in^2$
? = $(18in^2 + 30in^2 + 36in^2) \div 12in = 7in$

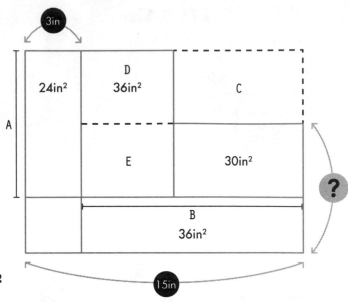

PUZZLE 55: 102in²

Create **rectangles A** and **B**
Rectangle A = $6in \times 14in - 26in^2 = 58in^2$
Rectangle B = $232in^2 - 58in^2 = 174in^2$
$174in^2$ = **A** x 3, so length **C** = $6in \times 3 = 18in$
Create **rectangle D**
$18in = 9in \times 2$, so **D** = $174in^2 \div 2 = 87in^2$
D + ? = $21in \times 9in = 189in^2$
? = $189in^2 - 87in^2 = 102in^2$

PUZZLE 56: 135in²

$39in^2 = 13in^2 \times 3$, so **length A** = $4in \times 3 = 12in$
Create **rectangles B** and **C**
B = $6in \times (12in + 4in) - 58in^2 = 38in^2$
C = $83in^2 - 38in^2 = 45in^2$
Length D = $35in - 12in - 4in = 19in$
Create **rectangle E** = $19in \times 6in = 114in^2$
E = **B** x 3, so **?** = **C** x 3 = $135in^2$

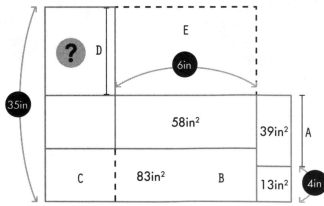

PUZZLE 57: **14in**

Length A = $72in^2 \div (7in + 5in) = 6in$

Create **rectangles B** and **C**

B = $7in \times 6in = 42in^2$

C = $5in \times 6in = 30in^2$

$7in + 5in + 9in = 21in$

Create **rectangle D**

$7in = 21in \div 3$

D = $75in^2 \div 3 = 25in^2$

$31in^2 + $ **B** $ + $ **D** $ = 98in^2$

? = $98in^2 \div 7in = 14in$

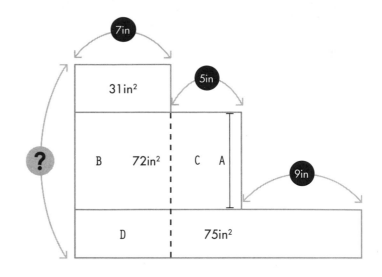

PUZZLE 58: **32in²**

Create **rectangle A**

A = $4in \times 10in - 25in^2 = 15in^2$

Create **rectangle B**

B = $4in \times (15in - 10in) = 20in^2$

A = (**B** $+ 25in^2) \div 3$, so **C** = $51in^2 \div 3 = 17in^2$

? = $15in^2 + 17in^2 = 32in^2$

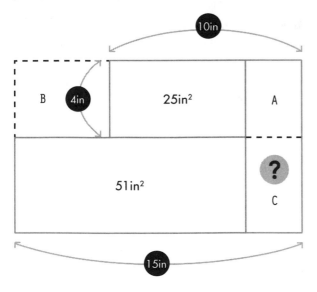

PUZZLE 59: **142in²**

Length A = $42in^2 \div 14in = 3in$

Create **rectangle B** = $9in \times 5in = 45in^2$

$35in^2 + 42in^2 + 26in^2 = 103in^2$

$9in = $ **A** $\times 3$, so **?** $+ 122in^2 + $ **B** $(45in^2) = 103in^2 \times 3 = 309in^2$

? = $309in^2 - 122in^2 - 45in^2 = 142in^2$

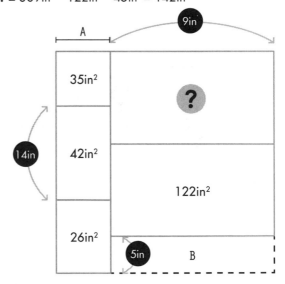

PUZZLE 60: 87in²

Rectangle A = 4in x 9in − 19in² = 17in²
Create **rectangle B** = 4in x 8in = 32in²
Create **rectangles C** and **D**
Rectangle B + 19in² = **A** x 3, so **rectangle C** = 12in² x 3 = 36in²
Rectangle D is the same height as **rectangle B**, so **rectangle D** = B + 19in² = 51in²
? = 51in² + 36in² = 87in²

PUZZLE 61: 35in

Create **rectangles A** and **B**
A + B = 52in² x 2 = 104in²
Rectangle B = 4in x 10in = 40in²
Rectangle A = 104in² − 40in² = 64in²
Create **triangle C** = 37in²
Create **rectangles D** and **E**
D + E = 67in² x 2 = 134in²
Rectangle E = 6in x 10in = 60in²
Rectangle D = 134in² − 60in² = 74in²
Triangle C + 37in² = **D**, so **length F** = 10in
Create **triangle G** = 48in²
48in² + **G** = 96in²
96in² is 150% of **rectangle A** (64in²), so **length H** is 150% of 10in = 15in
? = 10in + 10in + 15in = 35in

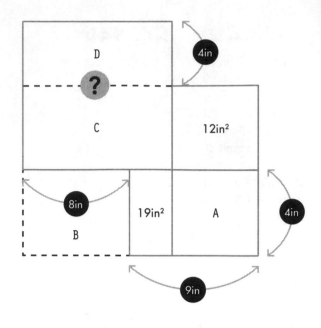

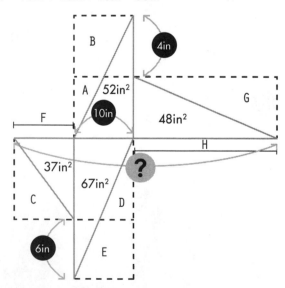

PUZZLE 62: 14in

Create **rectangles A** and **B**
A = 3in x 7in = 21in²
B = 45in² − 21in² = 24in²
Create **rectangles C** and **D**
27in² + **A** = **B** x 2, so 34in² = **C** x 2
C = 17in²
Rectangle D = 65in² − 17in² = 48in²
Rectangle D = rectangle B x 2, so **?** = 7in x 2 = 14in

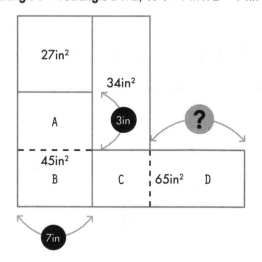

PUZZLE 63: 70in²

Create **triangle A** = 12in²
Length B = (12in² + 12in²) ÷ 3in = 8in
Create **rectangle C** = 8in x 9in = 72in²
Create **triangle D** = 35in²
Create **rectangle E**
Rectangle E + 35in² + **triangle D** = 21in x 9in – **rectangle C** = 189in² – 72in² = 117in²
Rectangle E = 117in² – 35in² – 35in² = 47in²
Rectangle E = 47in² rectangle at the top left, so
? = 35in² + **D** = 70in²

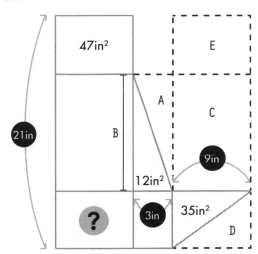

PUZZLE 64: 13in

Create **rectangles A** and **B**
A = 11in x 4in – 10in² = 34in²
Rectangle B is half the width of **rectangle A**, so
B = 34in² ÷ 2 = 17in²
Create **rectangle C**
Rectangle C is twice the width of **rectangle A**, so
C = 34in² x 2 = 68in²
? = (17in² + 34in² + 68in² + 63in²) ÷ 14in = 182in² ÷ 14 = 13in

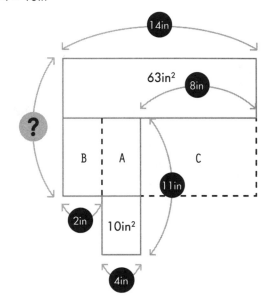

PUZZLE 65: 54in²

Length A = 42in² ÷ 6in = 7in
Length B = 7in – 4in = 3in
Create **rectangles C** and **D**
Length B = 9in ÷ 3, so **rectangle C** = **rectangle D** ÷ 3
Rectangle C = 15in²
Rectangle D = 45in²
? = 9in x 11in – 45in² = 54in²

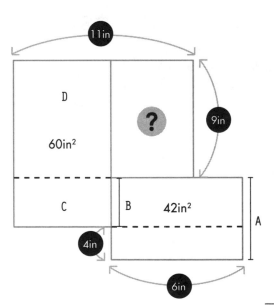

PUZZLE 66: 76in²

Create **rectangle A**
Rectangle A = 6in x 11in – 47in² = 19in²
Total width is 5in + 6in + 7in + 6in = 24in
Rectangle A is 6in wide, so **rectangle A** is a quarter of **?**
? = 19in² x 4 = 76in²

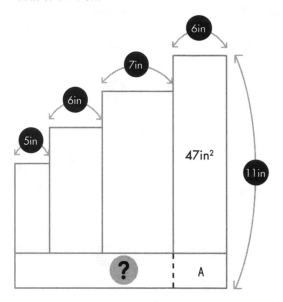

PUZZLE 67: 14in

Create **rectangles A** and **B**
A = 15in x 5in – 27in² = 48in²
B = 72in² – 48in² = 24in²
Create **rectangles C** and **D**
27in² = 54in² ÷ 2, so **rectangle C** = 48in² x 2 – 24in² = 72in² = **A + B**
Rectangle D = 105in² – 72in² = 33in²
Create **rectangle E** = **rectangle D** = 33in²
Overall width is 5in x 3 = 15in
? = (105in² + 72in² + 33in²) ÷ 15in = 210in² ÷ 15in = 14in

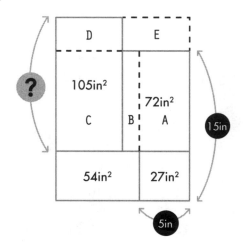

PUZZLE 68: 108in²

Create **rectangles A** and **B**
Rectangle A = 3in x 8in = 24in²
Rectangle B = 96in² – 24in² = 72in²
72in² = 24in² x 3, so length **C** = 3in x 3 = 9in
Length D = 9in + 6in – 9in = 6in
Create **rectangles E**, with area of 111in² and **F**, with area 135in² – 111in² = 24in²
Length G = 24in² ÷ 6in = 4in
Create **rectangles H** and **I**
Rectangle I = 9in x 4in = 36in²
Rectangle H is 9in wide, equal to **rectangle B**
Rectangle H = **rectangle B** = 72in²
? = 36in² + 72in² = 108in²

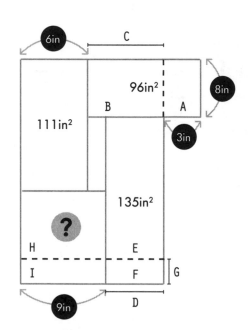

PUZZLE 69: 9in

Create **triangle A** and **rectangle B**
Triangle A = 28in2
Rectangle B = 116in2 − 28in2 = 88in2
Length C = 88in2 ÷ 11in = 8in
Length D = (47in2 + 28in2 + 116in2 +25in2) ÷ 8in =
216in2 ÷ 8in = 27in
56in2 + 43in2 + 30in2 = 129in2
43in2 = 129in2 ÷ 3
? = 27in ÷ 3 = 9in

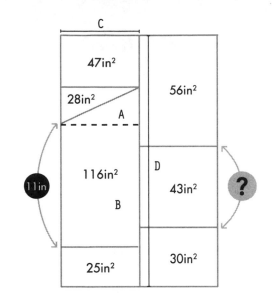

PUZZLE 70: 5in

Create **rectangle A**
Rectangle A = 19in x 8in − 96in^2 = 56in^2
Length B = 56in^2 ÷ 8in = 7in
Create **rectangle C**
Length D = 11in − 7in = 4in
Rectangle C = 4in x 8in = 32in^2
Create **rectangles E** and **F**
C = 32in^2 so **rectangle A** = **rectangle E** = 56in^2
Rectangle F = 154in^2 − 56in^2 − 56in^2 = 42in^2
Length G = 42in^2 ÷ 7in = 6in
Create **rectangles H** and **I**
H = 4in x 6in = 24in^2
Rectangle I = 54in^2 − 24in^2 = 30in^2
? = 30in^2 ÷ 6in = 5in

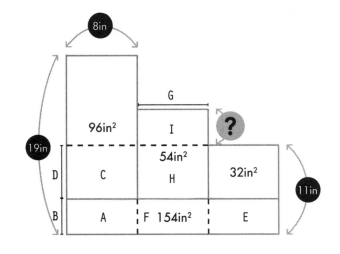

PUZZLE 71: 24in^2

Length A = 42in^2 ÷ 6in = 7in
Length B = 28in^2 ÷ 7in = 4in
? = 6in x 4in = 24in^2

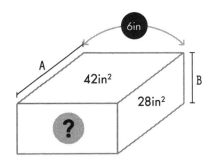

PUZZLE 72: 15in²

Length A = $12in^2 \div 4in = 3in$
Length B = $15in^2 \div 3in = 5in$
Length C = $25in^2 \div 5in = 5in$
? = $5in \times 3in = 15in^2$

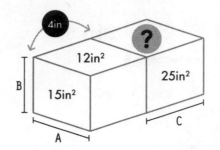

PUZZLE 73: 9in

Length A = $36in^2 \div 9in = 4in$
Length B = $24in^2 \div 4in = 6in$
Length C = $8in^2 \div 4in = 2in$
Length D = $33in^2 \div (9in + 2in) = 3in$
? = $6in + 3in = 9in$

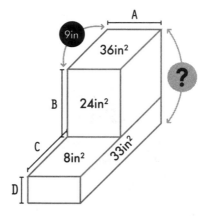

PUZZLE 74: 30in²

Length A = $15in^2 \div 3in = 5in$
Length B = $35in^2 \div 5in = 7in$
Length C = $7in + 3in = 10in$
Length D = $20in^2 \div 10in = 2in$
Length E = $8in - 2in = 6in$
? = $6in \times 5in = 30in^2$

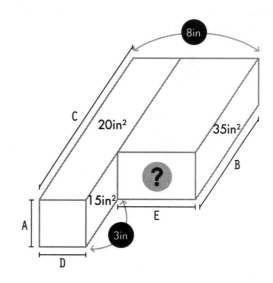

PUZZLE 75: 108in²

Length A = 48in² ÷ 8in = 6in
Length B = 54in² ÷ 6in = 9in
Length C = 18in² ÷ 6in = 3in
Create **rectangles D** and **E**
Rectangle D = 8in x 9in = 72in²
Rectangle E = 153in² − 72in² = 81in²
Length F = 90in² ÷ 6in = 15in
Length G = 81in² ÷ 9in = 9in
Length H = 15in − 9in = 6in
? = (6in + 6in) x 9in = 108in²

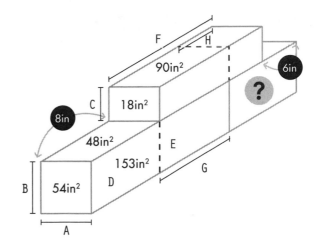

PUZZLE 76: 25in²

Length A = 24in² ÷ 6in = 4in
Length B = 20in² ÷ 4in = 5in
C = 6in x 5in = 30in²
D = 4in x 5in = 20in²
36in² = 18in² x 2, so ? = (30in² + 20in²) ÷ 2 = 25in²

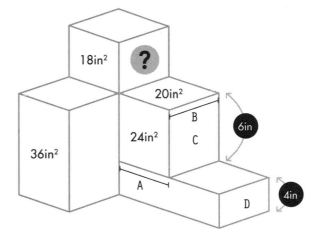

PUZZLE 77: 16in²

Length A = 24in² ÷ 6in = 4in
Length B = 48in² ÷ 8in = 6in
Length C = 72in² ÷ 6in = 12in
Length D = 12in − 4in = 8in
Length E = 8in − 6in = 2in
? = 2in x 8in = 16in²

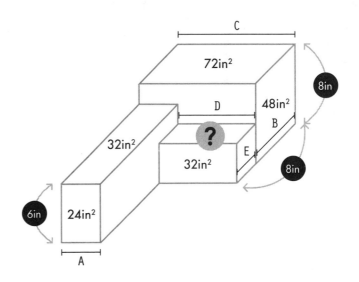

PUZZLE 78: 3in

Length A = $15\text{in}^2 \div 5\text{in} = 3\text{in}$
Length B = $12\text{in}^2 \div 3\text{in} = 4\text{in}$
C = $4\text{in} \times 2\text{in} = 8\text{in}^2$
Length D = $35\text{in}^2 \div (2\text{in} + 3\text{in}) = 7\text{in}$
Length E = $20\text{in}^2 \div (2\text{in} + 3\text{in}) = 4\text{in}$
? = $45\text{in}^2 \div (7\text{in} + 4\text{in} + 4\text{in}) = 3\text{in}$

PUZZLE 79: 18in²

Length A = $42\text{in}^2 \div 7\text{in} = 6\text{in}$
Length B = $36\text{in}^2 \div 6\text{in} = 6\text{in}$
Length C = $28\text{in}^2 \div 7\text{in} = 4\text{in}$
Length D = $B - C = 6\text{in} - 4\text{in} = 2\text{in}$
Create **rectangles E** and **F**
Rectangle E = $7\text{in} \times 2\text{in} = 14\text{in}^2$
Rectangle F = $20\text{in}^2 - 14\text{in}^2 = 6\text{in}^2$
Length G = $6\text{in}^2 \div 2\text{in} = 3\text{in}$
? = $3\text{in} \times 6\text{in} = 18\text{in}^2$

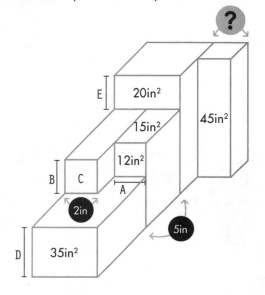

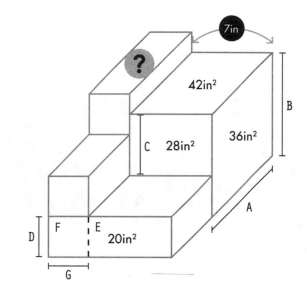

PUZZLE 80: 21in²

Length A = $28\text{in}^2 \div 4\text{in} = 7\text{in}$
Length B = $56\text{in}^2 \div 7\text{in} = 8\text{in}$
Length C = $48\text{in}^2 \div 8\text{in} = 6\text{in}$
Length D = $9\text{in} - 6\text{in} = 3\text{in}$
Length E = $33\text{in}^2 \div 3\text{in} = 11\text{in}$
Length F = $11\text{in} - 8\text{in} = 3\text{in}$
? = $7\text{in} \times 3\text{in} = 21\text{in}^2$

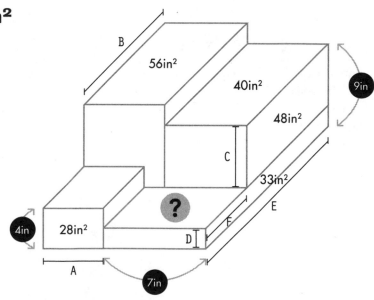